Successful Shepherding
Management + Preparation = Healthy Sheep

By
Darla Noble

Mendon Cottage Books

JD-Biz Publishing

Table of Contents

Introduction

Contrary to the opinions of many, sheep are an excellent choice when it comes to farming and raising livestock. Sheep are easily managed when managed properly and consistently (as should be the case with all livestock) and are profitable due to the fact that lamb is a highly sought-after meat.

But just like anything else, the profitability depends upon the quality of your product. You cannot expect to get top-market prices for sub-standard animals.

Knowing how to raise healthy, hardy sheep is the key to profitability. And know you will…if you take the time to become familiar with what lies within the pages of this book. By doing so you will be ready for lambing, be able to spot a potential problem before it becomes one and make management decisions that will make your flock stand head and shoulders above the rest.

Chapter 1: Pre-Lambing

Getting through the first lambing as a sheep owner is undoubtedly the biggest concern newbie shepherds have. Now while some breeds of sheep are more problematic during lambing time, the greater problem is the attitude of 'getting through'.

If you don't want lambing to be problematic then you shouldn't view it as such. Instead, you should see lambing for what it is:

*The natural growth of your flock

*A major part of being a shepherd

*A major case of when less is (usually) more

That being said, let's get down to the business of being prepared for lambing and making sure you (dare I say) enjoy it.

Choose the right breed

Some breeds of sheep are naturally hardier than others; meaning they require less intensive care, have an easier time lambing and possess strong maternal instincts. The breeds best known for having these qualities are the:

Katahdin, Dorper, Leiccster, Churro, Rambouillet, Montadale, Wiltshire Horn and most other meat breeds of sheep.

These breeds are known for their ability to consistently have twins and triplets, give birth to and raise their lambs with very few problems and for having a greater degree of stamina and resiliency.

Katahdin hair sheep—low maintenance, easy lambing, strong maternal instincts, excellent carcass value, hardy & healthy

Let your sheep be your teacher

A lot of beginners start with ewe lambs that are newly-weaned. They're smaller, cute and cuddly looking and new producers are under the false impression that buying lambs gives them more years of productivity before having to think about replacement ewes. I guess two out of three isn't too bad (they are smaller and cute and cuddly), but the truth of the matter is that ewes who have lambed a couple of times are far better for beginning shepherds.

Think about it. First-time moms aren't nearly as knowledgeable about pregnancy and childbirth as moms who've been-there-done-that, are they? So why would you think sheep would be any different? So when purchasing your first sheep, you will find it best to purchase three to five year-old ewes. These girls know what they are doing and will show you the way things are supposed to happen.

Experienced ewe cleaning her lamb. First one has been cleaned and is up ready to eat.

Buy quality ewes

Visit a few farms and attend a few farm shows before buying your sheep and whatever you do…BUY OFF THE FARM instead of from a sale barn.

Buying sheep directly off the farm allows you to see the overall condition of the entire flock, the management practices of the farm they come from and lets you know if what you are buying is a good representation of the flock or just the cast-offs (which you don't want).

Buying from the sale barn, however, is almost always an absolute no-no. Yes, there are those occasions when someone needs to disperse their flock of healthy sheep and chooses to go the sale barn route in order to get it over with. But more often than not, sale barn sheep are sheep that have health problems or are rogue for one reason or another. In short, when you buy from a sale barn you are most likely buying someone else's problems.

In the book, *Don't Be Dumb About Raising Sheep...Because They Aren't; The Basics of Raising Sheep,* you will learn what it is you are looking for when purchasing hardy, healthy sheep. But here's a brief re-cap...

*A straight topline

*A wide body (from top of the back to the belly

*A clean tail and rear (no wet or dried manure)

*Clean nose and unlabored breathing
*Strong legs that sit squarely on the four 'corners' with no limping or over-grown hooves

*No overbite

*An udder that is firmly attached and teats that are healthy (not warty, hard or too big for a lamb's mouth)

Breed purposefully
Knowing when to expect your lambs is a major step in the right direction toward successful lambing. A ewe's cycle is approximately eighteen days and they have a gestation period of five months. Some ewes will breed the first cycle they are exposed to a ram. Others require a second cycle. Therefore, when you put your ram in with your ewes you should expect the first lambs to be born within a six week period five to 6 months after exposure to a ram.

One ram can service (breed) up to fifty ewes easily.
Once you notice there is no activity going on between the ram and the ewes, you need to remove the ram and put him in a separate lot or field.

Some people leave the ram with the ewes clear through lambing. This is a mistake, though, because some ewes will breed back immediately and this is not healthy for your ewes.

Chapter 2: It's Time

Know the signs

As time draws near there will be visible signs in your ewes; signs that can alert you to the fact that lambs will be arriving soon. Some of these signs include:

*The udder will fill with milk and will be more visible. FYI: This is yet another reason to purchase ewes rather than ewe lambs when starting out, as this will usually not be noticeable in a first-time momma.

*The vulva will be swollen and pink in color.

*There will be a clear discharge from the vaginal area.

*A ewe will spend more time apart from the flock.

*A ewe will look hollow just below the hips because the muscles are relaxed and the lambs have 'dropped'.

When a ewe is actually in labor, she will:

*Usually separate herself from the rest of the flock.

*Paw at the ground and alternate walking in small circles with laying down.

*Lay down with her neck stretched out and head up in the air pushing and straining with each contraction until the lambs are born.
Once a lamb is born the ewe will begin licking the sack or lining off of it; usually starting with the face so it can breathe. But in the case of multiple births, she may not get this task completed before she lies down and delivers the next lamb. She may even walk off a bit to do so, but nine times out of ten she will not completely abandon the baby. She just needs a bit of space.

When the process is complete, healthy lambs will stumble to their feet and begin searching for nourishment from momma. They will likely be a bit clumsy at first and she may even be a little impatient at their clumsiness, but almost without fail instinct will prevail and nature will literally take its course.

Momma and triplets—healthy, bellies full and ready for a nap.

So where should you be while all of this is going on? Out of the way, that's where.

There are a few things you need to do once the lambs are on their feet and nursing. These will be discussed in chapter four. But the majority of the time a ewe can and will give birth without any assistance from you. You will know you need to step in and give assistance when any of the following occurs:

*The ewe is obviously contracting for more than two or three hours. If this is the case you need to quietly and calmly check to see if the lamb is breech or not presenting at all. Either way, working WITH the contractions you need to pull the lamb from the ewe. NOTE: An inexperienced shepherd will need another pair of hands; one to hold the ewe down in a firm but gentle way, while you do the work.

*You can see the lamb presenting incorrectly. FYI: lambs should be born in a diver's position—front feet/legs, followed by the head, etc. When turned wrong, you will most generally need to pull the lamb CAREFULLY and working WITH the contractions.

*The ewe is refusing to let her lambs suck. Sometimes this is simply a case of nerves (especially in first-time moms). She may even be 'suffering' from a case of poor maternal instincts. Moms of triplets need to be watched carefully, as well. She may be completely accepting, but three newborns are a lot to keep up with. Either way you need to put the ewe and her lamb(s) in a lambing jug (small pen approx. 5x5) and hold the ewe in place so the lambs can suck.

Ewe with triplets can be watched for a few days to make sure every one gets their fair share.

Other times she may have sore, chapped teats. You can alleviate this problem by massaging udder cream or lanolin on them after holding her for the lambs to eat.

*The lamb refuses to eat. Sometimes lambs are chilled or weak and don't have the energy to eat as soon as they should (within the first two hours after birth). Watching lambs to see that they nurse is the most important job you have when it comes to lambing. Seeing them nurse; getting that all-important colostrum is vital to their growth and overall health.

But beware! It's not enough to see them with their heads under mom's belly rooting around. You need to see actual sucking and tail wagging. You need to see full bellies and maybe even a bit of milk on their mouths.

Not eating within the first two hours is life-threatening to a lamb. They lose their body heat and become hypothermic. If this happens you need to take immediate steps to try to save the lamb explained in the section titled "Hypothermia".

Sometimes a lamb will refuse to eat no matter what you do. A lamb like this can be described as a 'failure to thrive' lamb. While the lamb will appear normal, there is likely something internally wrong; something that cannot be fixed. Nature knows this and sometimes a failure to thrive is simply nature's way of taking care of the inevitable early-on. This doesn't mean you shouldn't try to get a lamb to eat, but when several attempts fail, you need to realize that you cannot save every lamb. Sometimes it's just not meant to be.

Once your lambs are up and eating, however, the rest of your job is a matter of preventative care and good management. If you provide sound nutrition and safe living conditions, the sheep will take care of the rest.

Chapter 3: I Feel so Baaaad

Now it's time to go over the basics of the most common sheep diseases. Each one we discuss will cover the symptoms, treatment and prevention (not necessarily always in that order). Hopefully you won't experience all of these in your flock, but it would be unrealistic to say you will never have to deal with at least one of them. It's just always better to not have to use what you know than to not know what you need to in order to save your lambs.

Pneumonia

The most common ailment and killer of lambs is pneumonia. Pneumonia can come on quickly and is usually serious.
CAUSES and SYMPTOMS: While pneumonia is usually a bacteria, the primary cause s of pneumonia are damp, drafty living conditions with high ammonia content from urine and fecal matter.

As for the symptoms, the earliest sign is usually a lack of appetite. This will quickly be followed (if not caught and treated) by lethargy, labored breathing and a fever. You will also be able to hear the pneumonia when you hold the lamb close to you.

TREATMENT: Antibiotics is the only feasible treatment once pneumonia has set in. Small lambs are most susceptible to pneumonia, Some of the most effective antibiotics are NAXCEL and NUFLOR are the most effective, but in a pinch, LA200 and PENECILIAN will work. When giving an injection, it is important that you give it in the 'tent' of skin where the hind leg joins the body. NOTE: Even when it is instructed to give the medication in the muscle, don't. Just give it in the skin so you don't mar any cuts of meat. And yes, even a tiny injection given at just a few days or weeks will leave tough spots in the carcass.

PREVENTION: Keeping your lambs and their bedding dry is *the* number one preventative measure against pneumonia. Another important and oh, so easy thing you can do to prevent pneumonia in lambs is to give newborn lambs two or three drops of VetR$_x$® in each nostril within a few hours after birth. You will find it in the poultry department of farm and livestock supply stores. It comes in a small brown bottle and smells like pine cleaner, but most of all…it works. If you are experiencing, cold, wet conditions during lambing, you can repeat the dosage every other day or so for the first couple of weeks.

Coccidiosis

Coccidiosis is a disease that results from an internal parasite. The parasites are single-celled and attack the digestive system by damaging the lining of the small intestine. This makes it difficult for lambs and sheep to absorb nutrients from their food. The result is weight loss, poor growth and a lack of energy.

CAUSES and SYMPTOMS: Coccidiosis is almost always a result of poor management. Well, that and too much stress on the animals which could be accounted to poor management. Poor management resulting in coccidian infestations includes allowing the sheep to eat or drink from feeders and water tanks containing mud, fecal matter and stagnant water and over-crowding of animals.

Any of these conditions will cause stress, but the major stress factor that ignites an outbreak of coccidiosis is weaning. When weaning lambs from the mothers, it is ALWAYS best to move the adult ewes to a different pasture instead of the lambs; keeping at least one field between them. In other words, they should not be able to be side by side with only a fence separating them. This allows the lambs to retain some sense of familiarity with their surroundings (somewhat reducing the stress) and adds a bit of an out-of-sight-out-of-mind element. Oh, and don't forget to wean according to the signs of the moon.

Call me crazy, but I know from years of experience that this works. We would wean groups of 150 to 225 lambs at a time (depending on which flock we were working with). The bawling and bleating was always there for the first 24 hours or so if we went according to the moon. But the drop in their weight and other stress factors were almost non-existent (you will always have a couple that fall off). When we didn't wean with the moon, however, the noise level was significantly more, lasted longer and the lambs did not grow as well. They wouldn't eat as well and some would develop coccidiosis.

As for the symptoms, other than a loss of appetite, diarrhea is the main symptom—runny, watery, bloody diarrhea.

TREATMENT: The treatment for coccidiosis is relatively simple. Keep feeders and water tanks clean, provide clean hay or grass and treat their drinking water with Corid® (according to directions).

PREVENTION: Cleanliness and good management practices. That's it.

Clean barn

Eating from clean feeders

Other Parasites

To give you a complete overview of the different types of parasites would require at least one book dedicated solely to the subject. So for the sake of time and to spare you the boredom, we'll list the ones you need to be most aware of. Each one will be described and discussed briefly.

External parasites. The most common external parasites and diseases due to external parasites you need to be aware of are:

*Fly strike: blowfly maggot infestation on the flesh of sheep. These maggots are drawn to dirty wool (especially manure-fowled wool), wounds, runny eyes and foot rot. Keeping your sheep free of these things is your only real preventative measure. Fly strike is nasty, painful and usually deadly.

*Keds: reddish-brown fly that is often mistaken for a tick. Keds suck the blood from sheep; causing emaciation and anemia. Insecticides applied to the animal are the most effective treatment.

NOTE: Fly strike and Keds are not common problems with hair sheep, as neither parasite can easily cling to their short hair.

*Nasal bots: Yellow-gray fly bots that lay eggs in the nasal passages of sheep. The eggs hatch and make their way into the sinus cavities causing runny, snotty noses and poor appetites/weight loss. Applications of insecticides are the best treatment.

Internal parasites. Internal parasites are a danger to both the sheep and the shepherd. Left untreated, most internal parasites can kill sheep. Even when treated successfully, internal parasites can stunt the growth and development of sheep, cause ewes to be lacking in their ability to raise healthy lambs and ultimately cost the shepherd money.

The most common internal parasites (besides coccidian) are Haemonchus (barber pole worms) and Liver Flukes.

CAUSES: Internal parasites are caused by stress brought on by poor management, excessive heat/drought and lack of nutrition. Liver flukes are also caused by overly wet conditions where slugs and snails are prevalent.

SYMPTOMS: The symptoms vary according to the particular parasite. The symptoms of barber pole worms are loss of appetite, bottle jaw (the animal will have a knot under its lower jaw) and anemia. NOTE: You will know your sheep is anemic by checking their gums and underneath their eyelids. A bright red color indicates good blood levels and circulation. Medium pink to white indicates anemia—the parasite has eaten through the abomasum and is sucking the blood from the animal depleting it of both blood and protein.

The symptoms of liver flukes are diarrhea, blood loss (anemia) and weight loss.

I know—it sounds a lot like barber pole worms. This makes it difficult for even an experienced shepherd to be sure of the type of parasite. Fortunately, medications used to treat internal parasites are broad-covering. This means they can be used effectively to destroy a number of different parasites.

PREVENTION and TREATMENT: Let's start with the facts on this one. The most effective treatments for sheep against parasites are: CYDECTIN® IVOMEC® and VALBAZIN®. SAFEGUARD is also available but not nearly as effective. Some of these are used as pour-on mediations for some livestock, but for sheep, they should be administered orally.

Now let's look past the facts on *what* to use and talk about *how* to use these medications. Some shepherds are prone to over-use worming medications—much like people over-use antibiotics. In fact, if you are managing your flock properly you may never have to worm adult ewes.

Rotational grazing greatly reduces parasite infestations.

A major aspect of proper management is rotational grazing. By using rotational grazing to keep them from eating the grass down below 3 to 4 inches in height and by allowing 28 to 30 days to pass before putting them back into a pasture, you are doing everything possible to keep them from a) ingesting the worms which comes from the sheep's fecal matter and is on the ground and b) providing the larva from the worms a host (the sheep's intestines) before they die.

Other solid management practices include: feeding hay in feeders rather than off the ground OR feeding on the ground in different places each time and keeping the nutritional level of your ewes where it should be while they are nursing their lambs. It's hard work feeding lambs and they need extra calories, protein and energy to get the job done.

It is, however, wise to worm lambs when you wean them and then again in 28 to 30 days (to kill any larva). This helps the lambs adjust to grazing (and possibly feed) being their sole source of nutrition.

Pink eye
Pink eye is a highly contagious virus that simply has to run its course.

CAUSES and SYMPTOMS: The cause is a virus. The symptoms are red, watery, runny eyes. Some sheep will even go blind (usually this is temporary).

TREATMENT: There is no cure, but you can treat the discomfort they feel with a powder or spray you apply topically.

PREVENTION: Keep your sheep away from infected flocks.

Soremouth

Like pink eye, soremouth is a virus that is highly contagious.

CAUSES and SYMPTOMS: The cause is viral. The symptoms are painful sores around the mouth of the sheep. They look like blisters and scabbed-over blisters.

TREATMENT: There is a vaccine available but since it is a 'live' vaccine, it should not be used as a preventative, but as a treatment only. It has to be given in the wool-less part of the ear. Once used, it will have to be repeated yearly.

PREVENTION: Don't vaccinate against it in the hopes of preventing it, don't introduce it to your flock by bringing in a sheep that has or has had soremouth and don't mix your sheep with those that have had or have soremouth.

Chapter 4: Something is not Right

In addition to diseases caused by bacteria, viruses and parasites, sheep also experience illnesses brought on by their surroundings. It is important to know the ins and outs of the most common ailments sheep experience. Knowing what to look for, how to treat and (most importantly) how to prevent these things is paramount to your success as a shepherd.

Hypothermia
Hypothermia is the condition of body temperature dropping lower than what is necessary in order for the body's metabolism to keep things going. When this happens there is only one thing that will make things better—to raise the body's temperature back up to a point of being functional. This must happen QUICKLY in a lamb.

CAUSES and SYMPTOMS: The cause is simple—the lamb has not taken in the nourishment to keep it warm or has been exposed to extreme cold and wet rather than being nurtured and cared for by its mother.

The earliest signs that hypothermia is setting in include lethargy and weakness (the inability to stand). As soon as you notice this you need to stick your finger inside the lamb's mouth. If the lamb's mouth is warm and moist, you need to work diligently to get the lamb to eat. If the lamb's mouth is tepid, cool or even cold, time is of the essence.

TREATMENT: The first rule of treating hypothermia is to NOT feed the lamb. The warm liquid will adapt to the lamb's body temp instead of the other way around; causing more harm than good. Instead, you need to quickly raise the lamb's body heat by doing the following:

Place the lamb inside an old pair of sweat pants; allowing its head to stick out of one of legs and tying the other one shut. Next use a blow dryer on medium and high heat to heat up the sweat pants and the lamb from the waistband (pinching off the excess). Be sure to watch so that the blow dryer does not get too hot. Every two to three minutes, stick your finger inside the lamb's mouth to check its progress. As their temperature rises, you will also notice an increase in the lamb's energy level.

NOTE: You can achieve the same results by making a 'tent' out of a cardboard box; cutting a hole for the lamb's head and another one for the blow dryer 'tube' or 'hose'.

Some shepherds also treat hypothermia by submerging the lamb up to its shoulders in hot water (not hot enough to scald the lamb). They will drain the cooler water and add more hot water as needed until the lamb is no longer hypothermic. This works well, too, but the lamb must then be dried thoroughly with towels or a blow dryer to prevent a recurrence.

PREVENTION: Making sure your lambs eat within the first couple of hours of life and providing dry places for the ewes to give birth.

Bloat

Bloat is actually nothing more than gas; more gas being made than expelled.

CAUSES and SYMPTOMS: The gas build-up is usually caused by eating grasses that are too wet or too fine and/or feed that is ground too fine. The symptoms of bloat are relatively easy to detect: 1) distortion on the left side of their belly 2) foaming or frothing at the mouth.

TREATMENT: While bloat can be deadly, it usually isn't as long as you are watching for it. Usually a simple dose (1 to 2 tablespoons) of plain old mineral oil or even corn oil will do the job. If that doesn't work, inserting a stomach tube down their throat and into their stomach will cause them to belch and all will be well.

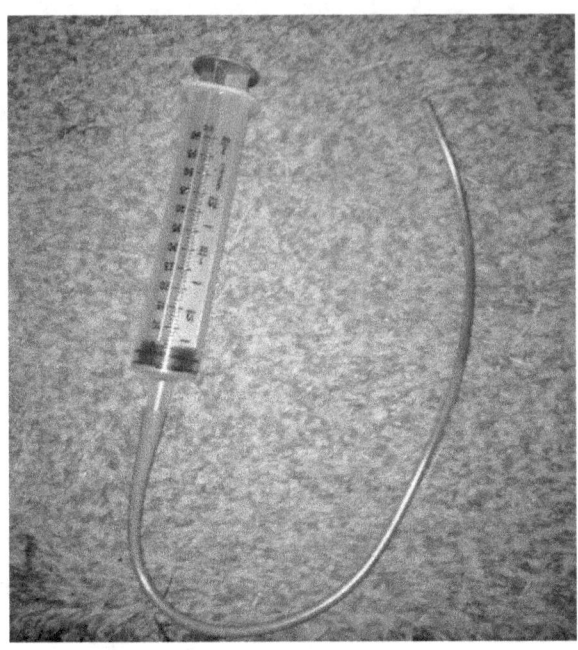

Stomach tube & large syringe for force-feeding & gas relief. PREVENTION: Feeding shell corn instead of cracked corn and pelleted feeds instead of dustier ground grains is always best. As for the grass, well, that's just something they usually adjust to on their own.

Acidosis

Acidosis is the condition of too much acid in the digestive system due to too much grain—specifically the rumen.

SYMPTOMS: The symptoms of acidosis are listlessness, stomach pain and depression (separating from the flock and lack of appetite).

TREATMENT: Treating sheep for acidosis should be done at the first signs, as it can prove deadly. Don't worry, though, it's not difficult. Baking soda water administered as a drench (oral medication) The amount is dependent upon the size of the sheep, but as long as you don't push the liquid into their lungs when you squirt it in their mouths, you really can't overdose them.

PREVENTION: Prevention is as easy as introducing grain or feed slowly and in small quantities. Grains should also be whole rather than cracked or ground.

Copper toxicity

Copper is a natural mineral found in the ground/grass and in mineral supplements given to livestock (especially cattle). Sheep are especially sensitive to copper—the excess being stored in the liver and ultimately causing damage.

SYMPTOMS: Weakness, lack of appetite and yellowish-brown skin and mucous membranes.

TREATMENT and PREVENTION: Treatment of animals with too much copper in their systems comes in the form of sulfates administered orally or injected. The prevention is simple—don't expose your sheep to copper other than what is naturally in the grass or ground. What is naturally found there is so minimal it will not hurt them.

On the other hand, it is important…no, vital that you do not feed mineral supplements or feeds that contain copper. Some feed salesmen and agriculturists will try to tell you that the mineral tubs or blocks (which contain copper) are safe for cattle and sheep. Don't believe them. Use loose mineral for sheep. Period.

Foot rot

Foot rot is caused by bacterial infection in the feet of sheep. It is highly contagious and hard to get rid of. Flocks with foot rot are considered to be leprous to others because it is so difficult to get rid of and because it greatly devalues the sheep.

CAUSES and SYMPTOMS: It's already been stated that the cause is bacterial. The symptoms are lameness, a foul odor from the feet, deterioration of the hooves. BUT not all sheep with foot rot are lame. They all, however, have an odor.

PREVENTION and TREATMENT: Preventative measures include keeping hooves trimmed, not confining them to standing in muck and mud and by placing water tanks and possibly even feeders on 'beds' of 1 to 2 inch gravel. Not only does the gravel act as a drain to keep moisture at bay, but the gravel also acts as an emery board of sorts. As the sheep repeatedly walk across the rocks, the rocks file or wear down their hooves; removing the problem of over-growth where bacteria can hide and grow. Using rock beds also reduces and even removes the back-breaking job of hoof trimming from your shepherding duties. Whew!

If you are unfortunate enough to be plagued with foot rot in your flock, treatment comes in the form of foot baths of liquid or powdered zinc sulfate. Other forms of treatment include vaccination of animals, treating the ground with zinc sulfate and culling animals that exhibit the worst cases.

NOTE: Do not, under any circumstances, bring new, clean sheep into the flock until you have this under control.

Mastitis

Mastitis is a hardening of the udder due to bacterial infection.

CAUSES and SYMPTOMS: The bacterial infection takes place when the sanitary conditions of the milking ewes are sub-standard, if the udder is injured or sometimes when the ewe produces excessive amounts of milk. The tendency to contract mastitis is also somewhat genetic. Symptoms of mastitis are: swollen, hot and hard teats. Ewes may also walk awkwardly because their udder is so full. A ewe with mastitis will not tolerate her lambs sucking, either.

PREVENTION and TREATMENT: To prevent mastitis keep their barns as sanitary as possible (dry and well ventilated). You should also be mindful of slowly decreasing the amount of feed ewes get toward the end of lactation. This will help them decrease their milk production; making it easier to dry them up when you wean lambs. As for treatment, strong antibiotics injected into the udder are almost always necessary as is catheterizing the teats to drain the mastitis out of them. This can be very painful to the ewe but it must be done.

NOTE: DO NOT allow the drained milk/mastitis to fall to the ground or anywhere else. Contain it to a bucket that can and must be sanitized thoroughly when you are done.
It will be best if you cull ewes with mastitis from your flock.

Toxemia

Toxemia is a metabolic condition afflicting ewes in the final weeks or days of gestation. It is nothing more than a serious drop in blood sugar which causes a severe lack of energy.

CAUSES and SYMPTOMS: The causes are a lack of nutrition, poor body condition (too thin or too fat) and ewes who are older and nearing their final years of reproduction. The symptoms of toxemia are weakness, lethargy and the inability to function.

PREVENTION and TREATMENT: In this case, prevention and treatment are the same; varying only by time. To prevent and/or treat toxemia, give ewes warm molasses water or orally drench them with molasses or propylene glycol.

NOTE: Giving ewes a bucket of warm molasses water within three or four hours of lambing is a great preventative measure and a well-deserved treat.

Prolapse
Prolapse is a term meaning internal body parts are pushed out of the body as a result of stress and/or injury. There are three types of prolapse which can occur in sheep: intestinal/rectal, vaginal and uterine.

CAUSES and SYMPTOMS: The general causes were listed above, but more specifically, prolapses are caused by being too fat, dusty feeds that cause coughing, poor muscle structure as ewes get older, hormonal imbalance and a number of other causes of physical pressure. The symptom is singular. Intestines, vaginal tissue or uterine tissue will be protruding or hanging from the vagina or rectum.

PREVENTION and TREATMENT: Prevention is best handled by: 1) providing quality feed and not making ewes 'climb' or reach above their normal stance to eat. 2) Keeping your ewes in good condition in regards to their weight. 3) Managing breeding by not breeding ewes before they are old enough (12 to 15 months). 4) Not breeding ewes back too soon (once a year is solid).

Treatment sounds a bit strange to many, but the truth of the matter is you need to wash the exposed parts with warm, soapy water, rinse with warm, clean water and push them back inside. You may need to put a prolapse harness on for a few days or (yes, I'm serious) use duct tape (making sure the ewe can still eliminate their waste) to keep everything inside. It also helps to keep the ewe confined in a smaller area and baby her a bit.

Ewes prone to prolapse should be culled from the flock.

Chapter 5: No Shepherd Should be Without a...

The title of this book 'screams' the importance of management and preparation...for good reason.

Throughout the pages of this book you've been instructed on how to prevent the most common diseases and afflictions sheep encounter. Most of these preventative measures will be taken care of 'automatically' if your management practices are as sound as they should be.

Yes, there it is again...the 'sermon' about how successful shepherding comes down to two basic things: management and preparation. I know, I've said that already, but it won't hurt you to hear it again...and again.

This is especially true when it comes to lambing since the quality of your lambs determines the quality of your growing flock (in quality *and* quantity) and your reputation as a producer of both market lambs for slaughter and breeding stock. So as promised in chapter one, here are the essential preventative measures to take when lambing; measures that take just a few minutes but can save you hours of work and a considerable amount of money and worry.

What is a lambing kit
When you start breeding your sheep you need to also start assembling your lambing kit. A lambing kit is a supply box of things you will need to use on every lamb born as well as a few things you will only use occasionally and some things you hope you don't need but having them on hand means the difference between life and death.

THE BOX you use should close securely, be somewhat waterproof and easy to carry. A tackle box or lightweight tool box works well.

EASY ACCESS is essential. It will do no good to have a lambing kit if you can't get to it when you need it. Installing an inexpensive metal cabinet in the barn is the perfect way to make sure your lambing kit is always close at hand. Besides, there are things you will want to have close by that don't need to go in the lambing kit and don't fit. This cabinet is the perfect place to house these items.

NOTE: The cabinet should be wall-mounted and high enough off the ground that sheep cannot reach it.

What is inside a lambing kit
The following is a list of items that should be ever-present in your lambing kit as *well as* an explanation of why and now to use each item.

*VetR$_x$®: Each new lamb should receive 2 to 3 drops in each nostril within a few hours of birth

*Sharp scissors: Pick up each lamb and snip its naval cord to a length of 3 to 4 inches.

*Iodine: After snipping the naval cord, hold the lamb out in front of you, letting its hind legs hang down. Pour some iodine on the navel to disinfect and coat it against dirt. NOTE: Some shepherds keep a shot glass or restaurant-style condiment cup in their kit. They put iodine in it and dip the naval cord a few times to coat it. This works well, too.

*Small plastic child's barrettes: Keeping two or three of these handy is wise just in case you clip a navel cord too closely. They work as clamps to stop the bleeding.

*Ear tagger and lamb tags: You should tag each lamb by placing an ear tag in the lamb's ear. Some shepherds use small lamb tags at birth and then add a larger sheep-sized tag at weaning. Either way is fine, but for the purpose of easy sorting and detection, you will be wise to place all ewe lamb ear tags in one ear and all ram lamb tags in the opposite ear.

Lamb with small ear tag.

Adult sheep tag.

Options worth considering: order lamb and ewe tags with corresponding numbers or order different colors for ram and ewe lambs (example: blue & pink).

*Small spiral notebook and pen: Record important information about each lamb and its mother. The information you need to record:

Mother's ear tag number; date of birth; sex of lamb; type of birth (single, twin, etc.); lamb's ear tag number; an 'x' or '✓' to show you've done everything.

*Rags: Rags for cleaning off membrane sack if necessary and to wipe your hands or any messes you make.

*Disposable gloves: You should always have a few pair on hand in case you need to re-insert a prolapse, handle more than one ewe's lambs at a time or any number of other tasks.

*A bottle of water: Having one in your kit will allow you to wash a ewe's prolapse in an emergency. You can also use the water to wash teats that are fouled and offensive to lambs.

Shelved items
The following is a list of items you should always have in hand 1) that won't fit into the lambing kit 2) for occasional use and 3) just in case.

*Powdered colostrum: For those times you have ewe that is stressed and unable or even unwilling to take her lamb or for lambs that become hypothermic, powdered colostrum is a must. Mix only what you need, though, as its shelf life once mixed, is very short.

NOTE: Do not feed a hypothermic lamb until you've raised its body temperature.

*Glass bottle and Pritchard® teat nipple. The screw-on nipple is just the right size and shape for little lambs. There is none better.

NOTE: You will need to clip the tip of the nipple with nail clippers to open it. You can check to see if you've got the right amount of flow by running water through it. It should drip slowly but easily without suction. As for the bottle, the bottles that work BEST are Yahoo® bottles. If you don't like the stuff, dump it, but you need the bottles on hand in case you have a lamb you need to bottle feed and for feeding the colostrum to.

*Milk replacer: A bag of sheep/goat milk replacer is always good to have on hand. It needs to be kept in the dry and sealed securely to prevent moisture and caking.

*Baby aspirin: You can treat both adult sheep and lambs with BABY aspirin for lameness, fever and soreness from wounds.

*Pepto-Bismol®: This stuff works GREAT on lambs which get scours (diarrhea) from too much milk the first few days. Just a little dab will do, though (1 to 3 cc depending on their size).

*Wound spray: This is best kept on hand and used when/if you have to trim feet.

*Hoof trimmers: By using rock beds around water tanks and selecting black-hooved stock, you will have to do little trimming, but you still need a pair on hand.

*Syringes: You need small syringes and needles for administering antibiotic injections if necessary and syringes w/o needles work for drenching lambs with oral meds. Larger syringes (10 to 15 cc) for drenching ewes and force-feeding weak lambs.

*Stomach tubes: These tubes fit onto the large syringes for force-feeding and for relieving gas that can lead to bloat.

*Antibiotics: If and when you need antibiotics for pneumonia, you will need them NOW.

*Halters for restraining and leading sheep.

*Wormer and worming gun: A worming gun allows you to dispense parasite control medication (wormer) quickly and easily.

*Bolus tube: plastic tube in which you insert a bolus, run the tube along the inside of their jaw and release the bolus down their throat so they cannot spit it out.

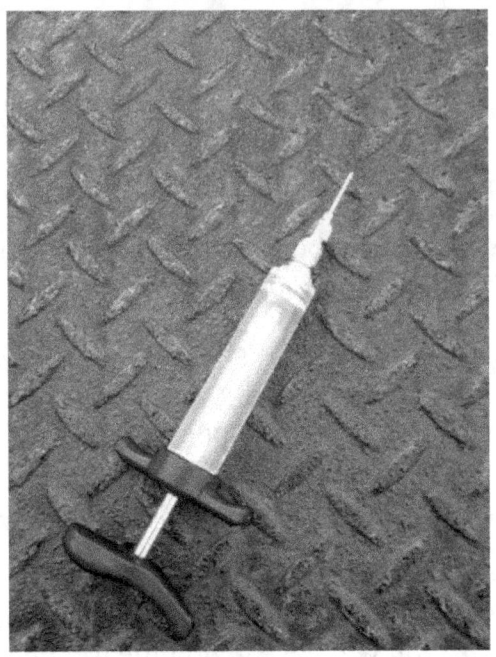

Syringe for administering antibiotics

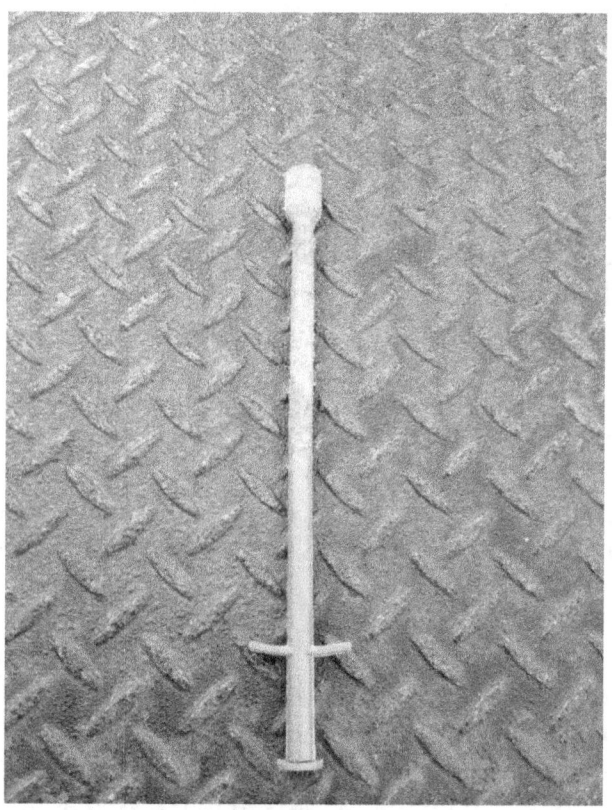

Bolus tube. Some medications come in bolus (pill) form and can be administered orally

Other essentials

Solid fencing, dry living conditions, clean water tanks and feeders and sound nutrition...all the comforts of home for a sheep. But there are also a few things you need to make shepherding easier, safer and more comfortable to you, too...

*Catch pen and chute: Whether it be weaning, worming or sorting, you need a place to easily catch and work with your sheep. Not only does it save time and stress on your sheep, but it saves you both physical and emotional stress. The catch pen and chute should be funneled; going from large enough to hold several sheep at once to funneling them down single file.

⟶ gate

*Shepherd's crook: Every shepherd needs a staff or crook to assist them in catching timid or frightened sheep. There is a bit of an art to using one, though, so stay calm and don't worry if you aren't a pro your first few times 'out'.

*Guard animal: Sheep are trusting, dependent, creatures of habit and yes, a bit nervous. But they are not dumb. Dogs and coyotes love to prey on their timid nature. Dogs do it for the purpose of mauling and 'sport'. Coyotes are after a meal. Having a guard animal-something to intimidate and fend-off predators is wise. Most shepherds use guard dogs—pyranese or maremma.

The key to successfully using dogs is to not make the dog your friend. Don't let them leave the pastures or barn lot. The less contact they have with you, the better.
Other options include llamas and donkeys. Both eat what the sheep eat which is a plus and both have proven to be good at their job.

Maremma dog guarding sheep.

Not all dogs, llamas or donkeys will serve you well and it may take a few tries to get a good guard. Just stay with it.

*Helpful sources: Everyone in the agricultural community needs reliable sources for supplies, information, education and networking.

Your local farm supply store will be able to fill many of your needs but other valuable supply resources include *Jeffers Livestock Supply* and *Mid States Sheep Supply.*

As for information, education and networking, align yourself with breed associations, your state's sheep producer association, department of agriculture, farm service agency, extension agency and regional farm show organizations.

There are also some excellent websites that provide good coverage on a number of topics pertinent to raising sheep. Some of the better ones include: http://www.sheep101.info/201/ and http://www.pipevet.com/sheep/sheep.asp.

Llama as a guard for sheep.

Conclusion

The popularity of raising sheep has been on the rise for the past two decades. The influx of ethnic groups into the United States who prefer lamb and sheep over beef has been the primary cause. Additionally, sheep have proven to be profitable weed eaters for dairy farmers and orchard growers.

No matter what the reason, though, sheep are an excellent choice for those who wish to raise livestock and contribute to the agricultural community.

For additional information on raising, managing and marketing sheep, you can contact co-author, Darla Noble, @ darlajnoble@yahoo.com.

Author Bio

Darla Noble is a native of mid-Missouri where she lives with her husband of thirty-three years, John. Darla's love of writing began in the fourth grade; after meeting up and coming children's author, Judy Blume,
who, by the way, autographed Darla's copy of "Are you there, God...it's me, Margaret".

Darla's love for writing and family makes her work sought after in the Christian market, parenting and family resources and ghostwriting for educators and inspirational speakers.

Health Learning Series

GRANDMA'S

NATURAL REMEDIES AND ANCIENT HERBAL BEAUTY RECIPES **Volume 1**

HEALTH LEARNING SERIES
DULEEP J SINGH AND J DAVIDSON

GRANDMA'S

NATURAL REMEDIES AND ANCIENT HERBAL BEAUTY RECIPES

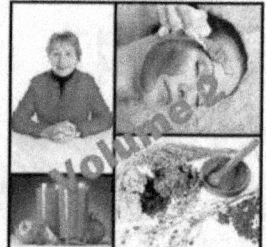

HEALTH LEARNING SERIES
DULEEP J SINGH AND J DAVIDSON

GRANDMA'S

NATURAL REMEDIES AND ANCIENT RECIPES

GRANDMA'S CURE FOR OBESITY
GRANDMA'S CURE FOR THE COMMON COLD

Volume 3

HEALTH LEARNING SERIES
DULEEP J SINGH AND J DAVIDSON

GRANDMA'S

NATURAL REMEDIES AND ANCIENT HERBAL RECIPES **Volume 4**

HEALTH LEARNING SERIES
DULEEP J SINGH AND J DAVIDSON

GRANDMA'S

HERBAL LORE

ANCIENT HERBAL RECIPES AND REMEDIES **Volume 5**

HEALTH LEARNING SERIES
DULEEP J SINGH AND J DAVIDSON

GRANDMA'S

ANCIENT BEAUTY REMEDIES FROM HER KITCHEN

Volume 6

HEALTH LEARNING SERIES
DULEEP J SINGH AND J DAVIDSON

GRANDMA'S

EASY TO USE TIPS

IN THE KITCHEN AND OUTDOORS **Volume 7**

HEALTH LEARNING SERIES
DULEEP J SINGH AND J DAVIDSON

GRANDMA'S

HOUSEHOLD HINTS AND RECIPES
USING TIME TESTED
ECONOMICAL TIPS IN YOUR HOME

75 Tips

Remove Stains

Peel Tomatoes   Perfect Pies

HEALTH LEARNING SERIES
DULEEP J SINGH AND J DAVIDSON

GRANDMA'S

NATURAL REMEDIES AND ANCIENT RECIPES

ALL 5 BOOKS IN 1

HEALTH LEARNING SERIES
DULEEP J SINGH AND J DAVIDSON

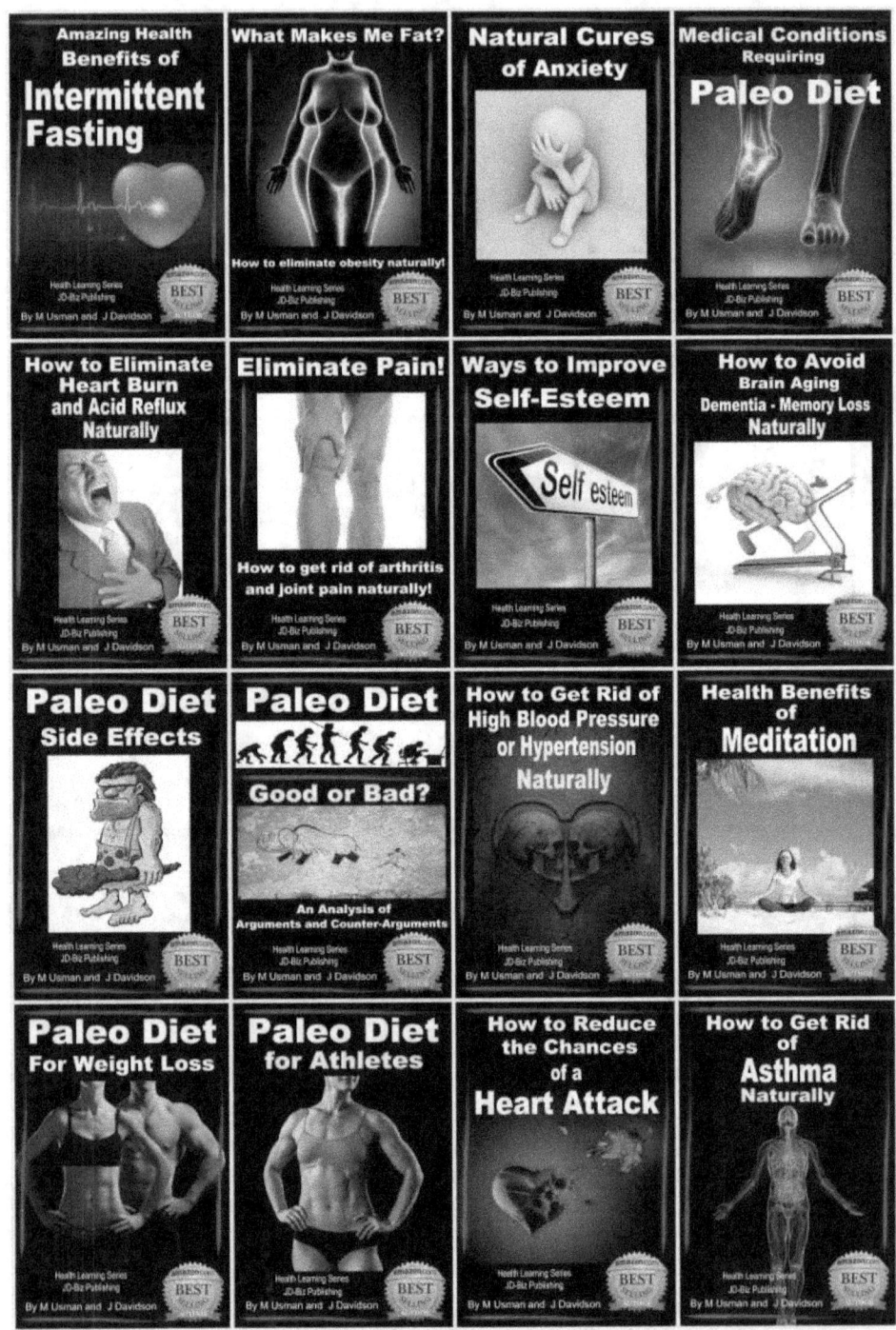

Amazing Animal Book Series

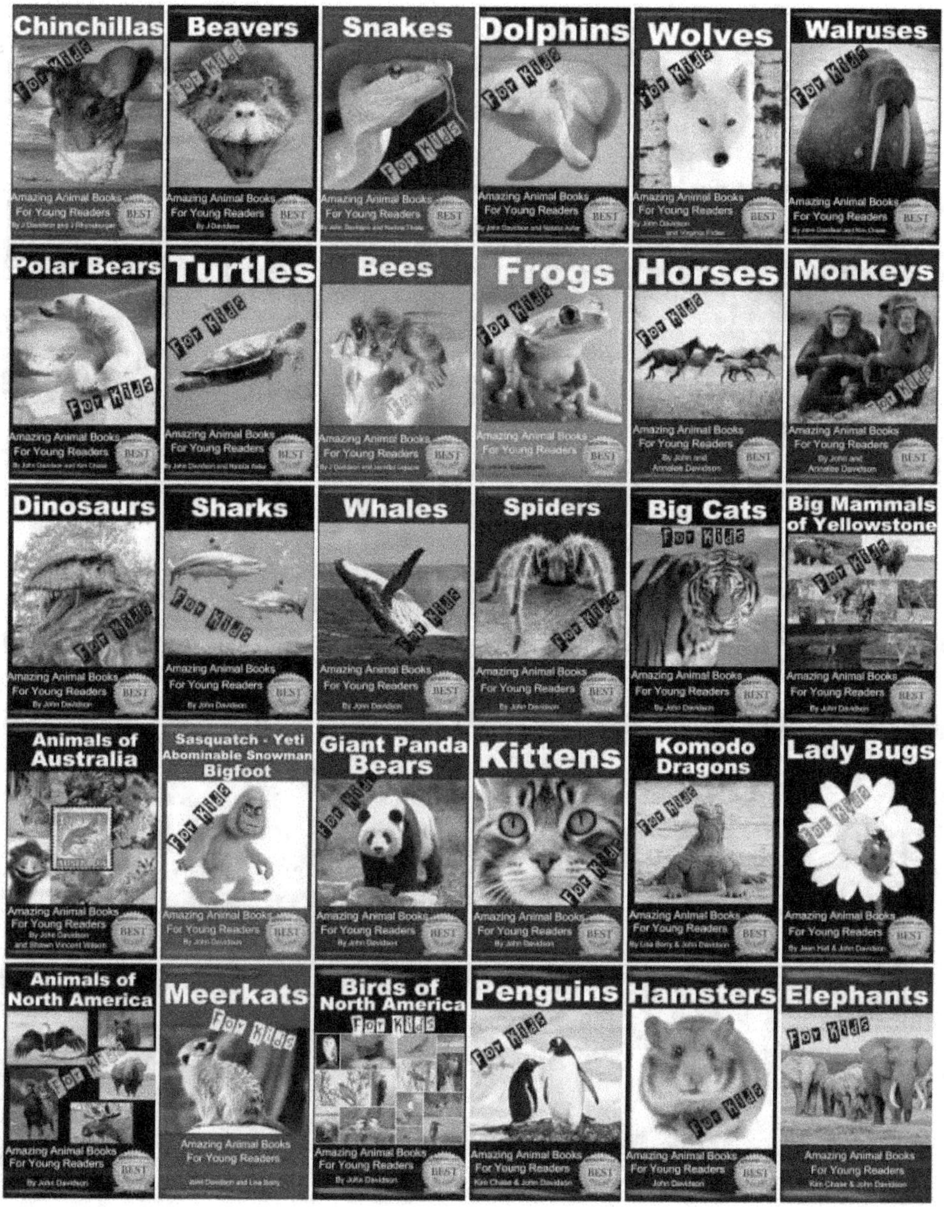
Chinchillas
Beavers
Snakes
Dolphins
Wolves
Walruses
Polar Bears
Turtles
Bees
Frogs
Horses
Monkeys
Dinosaurs
Sharks
Whales
Spiders
Big Cats
Big Mammals of Yellowstone
Animals of Australia
Sasquatch - Yeti Abominable Snowman Bigfoot
Giant Panda Bears
Kittens
Komodo Dragons
Lady Bugs
Animals of North America
Meerkats
Birds of North America
Penguins
Hamsters
Elephants
Amazing Animal Books For Young Readers

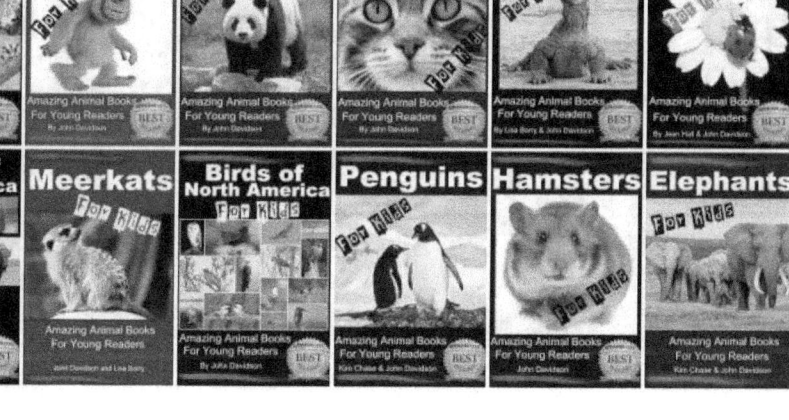

Learn To Draw Series

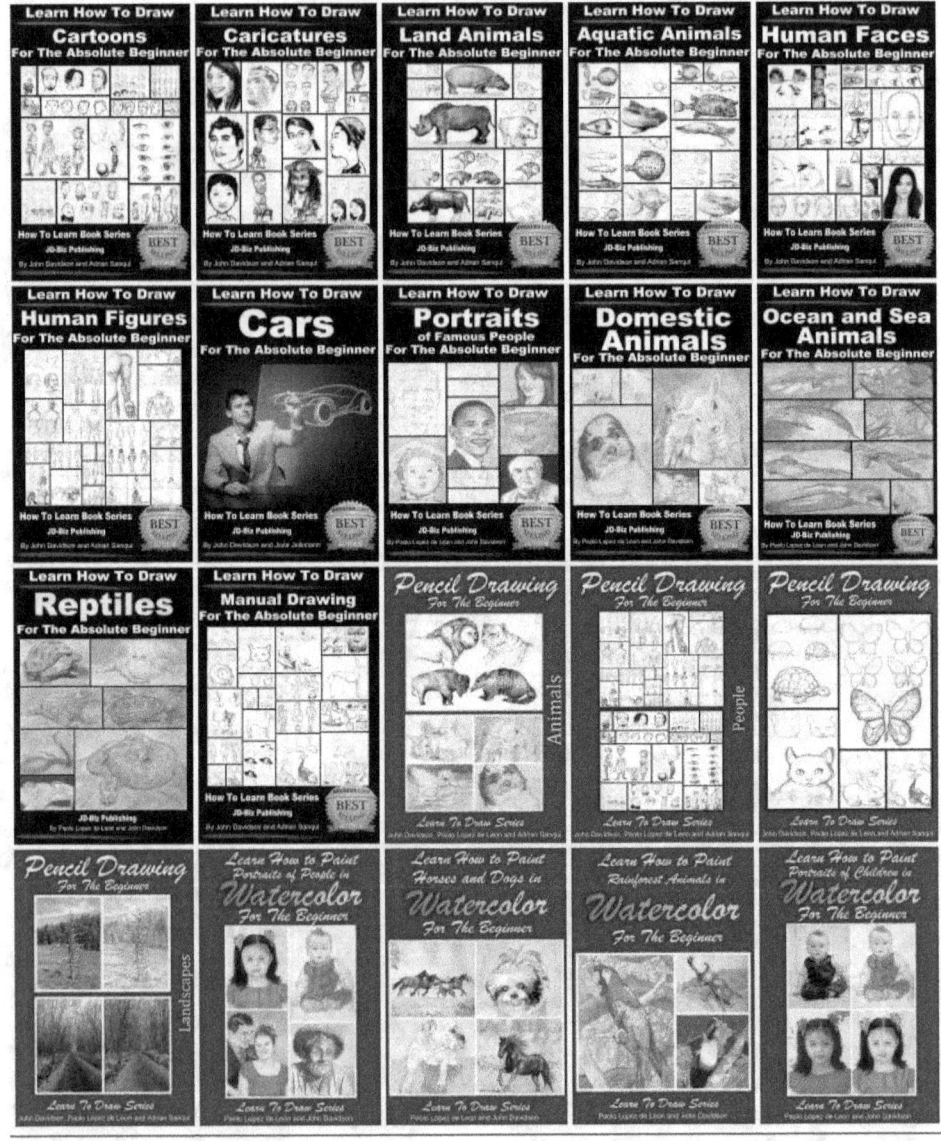

How to Build and Plan Books

Entrepreneur Book Series

Publisher

JD-Biz Corp

P O Box 374

Mendon, Utah 84325

http://www.jd-biz.com/

Mendon Cottage Books

P O Box 374, Mendon Utah 84325